TABLE OF CONTENTS

This book is all about how to train a dog using a dog whistle. A dog training whistle is a training aid that is especially useful for dogs in distance control such as hunting dogs. Whistles for training dogs stemmed from the need to train dogs to respond to a signal to return to the owner. They are more effective than your voice as they can travel over long distances, your dog can hear the whistle even when it is extremely windy or noisy and the sound from the whistle will not vary like your voice which may change depending on emotion.

Dog training whistles operate on a higher frequency than what the human ear can pick up but dog ears can. Even when there is a lot of other noise, the dog will still pick up the sound of the dog whistle as its ears are designed to resonate to sounds at a high frequency. Before you begin to use the training whistle, it is important that your dog has basic obedience training and can follow basic commands such as sit and stay so that you are able to train them on the whistle use.

The first thing to do is get a good whistle. You need to establish what sound will produce what reaction so that a particular sound is for a particular command. Ensure that you don't change the commands so that you do not confuse the dog. For example a short blow will be sit while a longer one will be for recalling the dog. Once you have established the commands, you can start by using the whistle to call the dog for a meal. If you have someone to help you let your helper hold the dog and when you blow the whistle, he can release the dog so when it comes towards you, you give it a treat or a reward and you praise and pet it.

When the dog associates the whistle pip with the command, now move to a greater distance and then blow the whistle and when it comes running to you, you reward the dog. As the dog masters the command and the responsive action, then you can move on to a field. Command the dog to sit or stay, move to a far distance and blow the whistle so that the dog will come to where you are. Repeat the actions so that the dog responds and will run to you when you blow the whistle. Do not take the dog for a long walk and release it until you are sure that it will obey the whistle signal.

HOW TO TRAIN A DOG USING A DOG WHISTLE

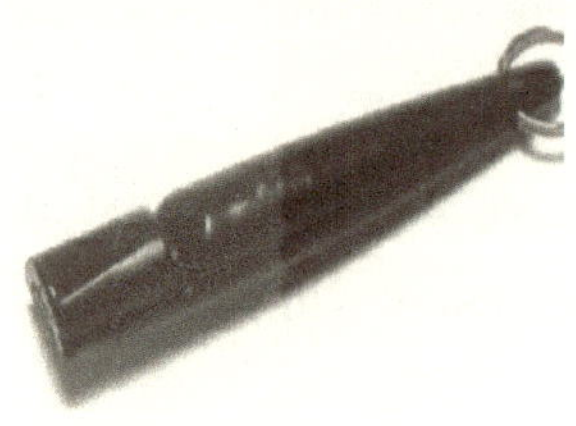

Dog whistle training is largely misunderstood. Can you believe there are some people who believe dogs are inherently able to understand that a whistle means to come back? Many of us have seen the fine work performed by sheepdog handlers and the exceptional level of whistle control they have with their dogs.

I started to train my first dog from the moment he came home with me. It was fun. It was, if I'm totally honest, pretty easy, too. He was a Labrador and his eagerness to learn and please me made training him fun, enjoyable and almost without exception, flawlessly simple. Then he grew up. Things began to change. Luckily for me, I discovered the most important dog training tool I've ever used. I swore by it then, I still do now.

As a puppy, I taught him to do lots of things. Sit, stay, come back, walk to heel, lie down, bark on command, give a paw – all, so much fun, so easy to accomplish.

Then, almost overnight, he started acting like a teenager.

Probably because he was one!

More worryingly, I had moved him on to a point where I actually wanted to compete with him in working tests and trials.

He had everything in his locker; he was fast, strong, intelligent, and REALLY intelligent and he loved to work.

But his recall was – at best 50/50.

If I'm totally honest, he'd only ever recall if the level of distraction and temptations around him were minimal.

Fortunately for me, I was learning the art of whistle training.

Fortunately for me, every dog I've ever trained since - regardless of breed, regardless of discipline, regardless of exactly what level the dog was at –

have ALL been trained using a whistle.

It's only now; at a point where I know more of the theory of canine learning that I appreciate just how and why whistle training is so incredibly potent.

The whistle, you see, is constant, consistent, emotionless and incredibly easy to operate – you don't even need to charge it up, follow an instruction manual or get a new one every other month.

They cost less than a tenner, yet I still have the same whistle I used 10 years ago and which has been utilized to train hundreds of dogs.

I won't go in to the technicalities of how to teach whistle training right now (that's something for later!) but I will happily explain some of the principles that make the whistle so incredibly valuable:

Dog Whistle Training: Why It Works

- A whistle can be used by ANYONE! Now I know that seems obvious, but think about it. Most family dogs have many different voices in their ears, day in day out. A whistle sounds the same whoever is blowing it. Whether it's a child or the dog's owner, the dog trained to recall to a whistle will do so regardless of who is blowing it. Although there ARE ways in which you can make your whistle recall unique to you.

- A whistle lacks emotion. Ever tried to recall your dog when you're in a panic? Or a hurry? Or even when you're a bit angry? Think your dog can't tell? Think again! A whistle lacks emotion and it is consistent – something which is absolutely crucial to successful dog commands.

- The sound of a whistle carries a long way, not everyone's voice does. Besides, nobody wants to be the person at the park who's bellowing at their dog to come back. A whistle is a sharp, sophisticated way to communicate with a dog outdoors.

- Dogs love the whistle. If trained properly, the sound of whistle can be as exciting to a dog as the sound of the biscuit tin being opened (yes, THAT exciting!). Believe me, my dogs go absolutely mad for the sound of the whistle and there is nothing – absolutely nothing – in the world that prevents them recalling when I blow that whistle. Don't believe me?

Using a whistle you can:

- Have a bullet proof, 100% recalls
- Ensure your dog is safe, off the lead in public
- Impress all of your dog-owning friends with a dog that comes back, first time EVERY time!
- Teach your dog to stop and stay at a distance
- Achieve almost 'sheepdog handler' like control of your dog, regardless of breed
- Have a simple, easy to follow dog training system that you can apply to ALL of your dogs, now and in the future

But before we move on to achieving 'Total Recall', you need to make sure you are properly equipped.

HOW TO TEACH YOUR DOG TO COME BACK USING A WHISTLE

I will keep this short, simple and to the point – because this really doesn't need to be over complicated.

Step 1: Associate the whistle with GREAT things.

What I mean by this is, get the dog used to hearing the sound of the whistle ONLY when something fun and exciting is happening. For example, you could use the whistle when the dog is about to be fed. You could use the whistle when you are about to take the dog out for a walk, basically, whatever it is that your dog loves, use the whistle to get them to associate great things with that sound.

Step 2: Use the whistle in the home to begin with.

Wait for an opportunity when your dog is calm, give several tweets on the whistle and reward lavishly when he comes back to you. Do this sparingly. You need the dog to succeed. Don't set the up to fail. This isn't a challenge.

Step 3: Use the whistle when the dog is in the garden at a point where he's not paying attention to what you're doing.

Give several short, sharp tweets on the whistle and even consider running off in the opposite direction so he chases you. Again, reward well. You can move this step to using the whistle to call the dog for his dinner. He will begin to associate the whistle sound with great excitement and something worth returning for.

Step 4: Use the whistle in public, but in a confined area.

Only use the whistle at a stage where the dog is not running away and is MOST likely to return to you. Again, you are not trying to set the dog up for failure, you want him to succeed. When he recalls to you, reward

Step 5

Begin to use the whistle (again, only sparingly – NEVER over use the whistle while you are in the early training phase) when the dog is further away from you in a public place but when there is NO distractions which are likely to make him 'fail'.

The process is to use the whistle as the single recall device when you're out with your dog. But remember, to condition your dog first to get used to the sound of the whistle and have the dog make the association between the whistle sound and very good emotions. Imagine this, if you have a dog that reacts positively to the sound of the fridge door being opened, you could use the whistle at the same time as opening the fridge door – the dog will associate one sound with the other.

You are trying to achieve a reaction from your dog which makes the sound of the whistle so overwhelmingly positive, they will want to come back to you.

Always reward lavishly, particularly in the early stages of training.

If the dog does not come back for any reason STOP whistling, the last thing you should do is simply stand there whistling away and have the dog ignore you – that's a disaster and would also suggest that the foundation sound-association work hasn't yet been properly put in place.

When you have reached a point in your training where the dog understands and consistently responds to vocal commands it is a good time to introduce the whistle. If you are having trouble with the verbal commands there is really no reason to throw a whistle into the mix and confuse the dog. They absolutely have to know the basics verbally to continue training with a whistle. It is a crawl, walk, run type of situation as any other training and only by overlaying the whistle with commands that are already understood will it be effective.

Introducing the whistle is a simple process when done correctly and it is also a quick process if you are consistent with your dog. Have the dog on a leash or check cord so that you still have control over the situation if you need to make corrections. There are a few basic whistle commands that are universal and that is: one blast = sit, three or four repeated blasts = here/ come, and one long trill noise = change direction. I do not train with any more than these three commands because you want to keep it simple just as many other trainers will tell you. When you have your dog walking at "heel" and you give the "sit" command follow it immediately with one blast of the whistle. You can start with each time you give the sit command blow the whistle, then every other time give the verbal command, and eventually the dog will understand that the verbal and the whistle command mean the same thing. Consistently do this in sessions until you have slowly dropped the verbal command all together. For the "here/come" command it will work the same way. When the dog is retrieving introduce the 3-4 blasts as they make their way back to you while still giving the verbal command. Just as with the "sit" sessions slowly drop the verbal command until it is no longer needed. The same consistency is needed to make your "turn/change direction" command into the long trill sound of the whistle so you can give them your hand signals and show them where they need to go. This training could take anywhere from 5-6 days or up to 2-3 weeks depending how fast your dog responds and especially on how consistent you are with the training.

Now, before any of this training you must be able to choose the right whistle. There are many different ones available and everyone has their favorites. I work with the FOX 40 Classic Whistle and the FOX 40 Mini. They are both a pealess design whistle which makes them perfect for many of the hunting situations we are in. On days where the wind is blowing a million miles an hour and it is freezing rain these little whistles will truly hold up. They are loud enough to be heard over the wind, rustling corn stalks, and water interferences. The pealess design means there is no cork ball inside the whistle to make its sound and this is why it has no chance of freezing up from saliva blown into the whistle.

We use the Roy Gonia Whistle for short distance training, starting young pups, and out in the field when there isn't too much interference noise. These whistles are not quite as loud and work perfectly for those situations. The other whistle I would recommend is the Roy Gonia MEGA Whistle which is much louder for noisy situations and it directs the sound out to the dog. It does not allow the sound to go back or to the sides and protects the handler's ears.

The Acme line of whistles is the oldest in the world and they have pioneered many of the whistles used today. I do recommend looking into other whistles such as these: Acme T2000 Pealess Tornado (one of the world's most powerful whistles for extreme conditions/high interference), Acme Silent Dog Whistles (used by many people who cannot handle the sound of training with whistles: very LOUD to dogs very QUIET to people), and the Dual Tone Whistles (able to make the trill and sharp blasts all in one whistle). I believe the Acme, FOX 40, and Roy Gonia whistles are the top three brands to choose from and are the most highly recommended by all trainers. It will come down to personal preference and what whistle is going to fit your hunting/training situation.

HOW TO USE A DOG WHISTLE

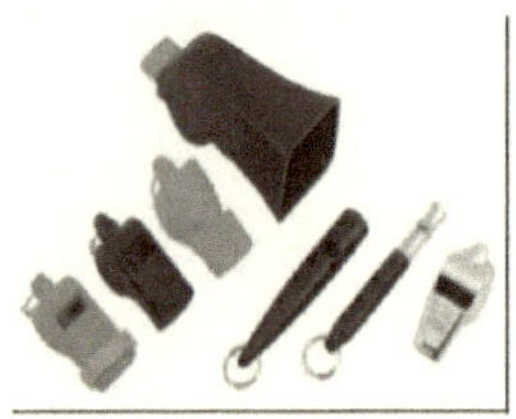

Dogs are man's best friend and will give their life if their master is in danger. Dogs will obey you and serve you if you train them well. Training your dog for is not as easy as you may think, though. You will need a lot of patience and determination before your dog learns all the things that you want your dog to do. Capturing your dog attention's during your training is the hardest part that is why a lot of dog owners are using a device to get their dog attention.

This device is called a dog whistle. Dog whistles have been used by many dog owners for a very long time. The whistle works by producing a high pitch frequency sound that only dogs can hear. By using a dog whistle, you can train your dog to respond to the sound that will be emitted by the dog whistle. Here's how you can effectively use the dog whistle.

- **Test your dog whistle**. Upon purchasing a dog whistle, try to puff on it and listen to the sound it will emit. The sound that comes out from the whistle is caused by the force of the air of the metal tube because the sound of the dog whistle is only audible by dogs, not by humans.

- **Observe the effect of the sound to your dog**. To properly test the dog whistle, wait for your dog to fall asleep and softly blow the whistle on your dog. A dog whistle contains a screw and a nut where you can adjust the frequency if it is turned. Try to test its frequency until your dog wakes up so you will know what level of frequency your dog can hear. Make note of that frequency because it will be the frequency you will always use to capture your dog's attention.

- **Use your dog whistle**. After knowing what level of frequency your dog hears, it is time to use your dog whistle as a device to teach your dog to listen and pay attention to the things you will teach. Try to use the dog whistle with different sequences. For instance, one long whistles means stop while a short whistle means sit.

- **In teaching your dog, make sure you are consistent with your whistle frequency so your dog will know what specifically you want your dog to do**. In case you have a lot of dogs, buy a dog whistle for each of your dog so your dogs will not get confused by the sound of the whistle that they will hear. If possible try to put a name tag on each whistle so you will know what dog whistle you will use. Make sure to use the correct dog whistle for each of your dogs.

Dogs are loveable and trainable by nature; but it will take time before they get used to the sound of the dog whistle. It will also take time before they perfectly follow the commands that you want them to execute. So make sure that after your training session with your dogs, pamper them with love and care that they deserve.

Did you know that your dog's hearing is a lot better than yours? Have you ever wondered why sometimes he seems to be barking for no reason at all? Maybe he's hearing sounds that you can't hear. A dog whistle, for instance, produces an ultrasonic sound that humans can't hear but dogs can.

This silent whistle comes in handy when Fido is behaving badly. Just like clapping your hands, stomping your feet, shaking a can of coins or squirting him with water, the high-pitched whistle can stop him in his tracks and get his attention without bothering your neighbors.

- Observe your dog closely so you can stop him the moment he starts behaving badly.

- Blow the dog whistle as soon as your pet companion starts chewing on an inappropriate item, jumps on the sofa, digs up the yard or displays other undesired behavior. The sound of the whistle hurts his ears so he'll stop whatever he's doing.

- Praise your dog for stopping the undesired behavior and let him go about his business, but keep watching him like a hawk.

- Blow the whistle again if your dog continues the undesired behavior and praise him when he stops. This time, redirect his attention -- give him a chew toy if he was chewing an inappropriate item, bring him to his pet bed if he was about to lounge on the sofa, or walk him to his digging pit if he was digging in an area that's off-limits.

- Throw a party for your pet when he displays good behavior. Hug him and give him treats to reinforce the good behavior. Be consistent and keep using the whistle each time he displays the undesired behavior. Over time, your dog will associate his bad behavior with hearing the unpleasant sound of the whistle and his good behavior with getting hugs and treats. It'll motivate him to keep displaying good behavior.

A silent dog whistle is an effective training tool that comes handy in a variety of situations. Because dogs are equipped with an acute sense of hearing, silent dog whistles are a great way to train dogs over distances.

Owners of hunting dogs, herding dogs or simply owners who want to teach their dogs commands from a distance may benefit from using a dog training whistle to train their dogs.

Dog whistles can also be used in situations where a dog can't hear you due to noise.

There are a variety of dog whistles on the market and choosing the best depends of a variety of factors. And despite its name, this training tool can also be used to train other animals, including cats.

Facts about Dog Whistles

A silent whistle is often referred to as Galton's whistle to honor Sir Francis Galton who first invented it. Francis created the dog whistle in the 1876 for the main purpose of studying the different ranges of frequencies animals could hear.

A dog whistle is typically in the range of 16,000 Hertz to 22,000 Hertz. Humans are believed to perceive 20 Hertz to 20,000 Hz, whereas the hearing range of dogs is believed to be between 40 Hertz to 60,000 Hertz.

The sensitive ears of dogs were specifically designed to hear higher frequencies because such frequencies are emitted by small prey such as rodents.

As the name implies, a silent dog whistle is capable of producing sounds at higher frequencies than those perceptible by humans, but well within the dog's range. You can blow through a silent dog whistle and hear the air blowing through it, but often without hearing a sound. However, a dog training whistle may also emit frequencies as low as 16,000 Hertz which are audible by humans.

How to Use a Silent Dog Whistle in Training

Silent dog whistles are a favorite among gun dog owners who can rely on their ultrasonic whistles to deliver commands from a distance even in heavy cover or on days with high winds.

This is an effective training tool since it will get the dog's attention without the need to shout over long distances or when the dog is out of sight. If you are interested in training your hunting dog or herding dog to obey to a silent dog whistle, you will need to practice a bit before you and your dog get it right.

It is often erroneously assumed that dogs automatically respond to the noise emitted by a silent dog whistle with no previous training. There is no truth to that. The noise of a whistle to a non-whistle trained dog is the same as the noise of a dog clicker by a non-clicker trained dog.

Dogs require training in order to respond to commands delivered by a whistle, but dogs that are already trained to respond to verbal commands or hand signals will catch on quickly with the right training.

How to Train a Dog to Respond to a Whistle

The different tones produced by the silent dog whistle will basically become cues just as with verbal commands or hand signals. A dog who has mastered verbal commands or hand signals can be switched over to whistle commands with the proper training.

The best way to accomplish this is by asking your dog the familiar verbal command or hand signal followed by the new whistle command. After repeating several times, the verbal command or hand signal can be gradually phased out and replaced by the silent dog whistle command. It is very important to be consistent and use the same type of whistle tone for specific commands. You are virtually free to select any type of whistle command as long as you stick with the same ones. Of course, it is much easier on the dog if each whistle command is quite unique to avoid confusion. Clarity, consistency and patience are virtues necessary to switch a dog over to whistle commands.

Some Examples of Whistle Commands

While you are free to select the whistle blasts that you prefer, there are some "standard" commands. For instance, if you wish to switch your dog over from verbal commands to whistle commands, you may want to follow these easy steps.

Training Sit

1. With your dog in heel position, ask your dog to sit using your verbal command
2. Immediately sound one long whistle blast while keeping your hand raised and open
3. Upon sitting, give verbal praise followed by a dog treat
4. Repeat over and over
5. Drop the verbal command and start giving it every other time
6. Once your dog seems to grasp the concept, drop the verbal command completely

Training Come

1. When your dog is at a distance, call your dog using your verbal command
2. Immediately sound a series of whistle pips as you keep your arms stretched out to the side
3. When the dog is next to you, give verbal praise followed by treats
4. Repeat over and over
5. Drop the verbal command and start giving it every other time

Once your dog seems to grasp the concept, drop the verbal command completely.

HOW DOES A DOG WHISTLE WORK

Dog whistles exploit the difference between the hearing range of a dog and that of a human. They use a pitch that is too high for humans to hear but is high enough for dogs to hear. Longer whistles have lower pitches, so in order to get a higher sound; dog whistles use a very short tube (only about an inch long and possibly shorter).

Because humans cannot hear in the range of a dog whistle, the person who is blowing it will hear only the hissing of the air through the whistle. As a result, dog owners can train their dogs while other people are around without disturbing them. A dog whistle is effective at getting a dog's attention because there are very few sounds that occur at that range in a dog's hearing. Despite the name, dog whistles work on cats as well.

The human hearing range extends from 20 Hz to 20 kHz. A dog's hearing range, on the other hand, normally extends to 45 kHz, while a cat can hear as high as 64 kHz. Because of this difference, dog whistles are constructed to make sounds between 23 kHz and 54 kHz.

Dog whistles are also known as silent whistles or Galton's whistles.

A whistle-trained dog is easier to handle at a distance, in heavy cover, and when the wind is high. Whistle commands also keep from alerting game like verbal commands.

All three brands are high-quality products and come in many different styles and designs.

- Most of the whistles we sell are made of **high density plastic**. We also have a few styles in metal.

- These whistles are all **well-made, high-end products**. These whistles are not only the standard in dog training but they are also used around the world by professional and amateur referees for all major sporting events.

- **Whistles with a Pea**. Many of the dog whistles we sell have a "pea." The pea is the cork ball inside the whistle. Having a pea allows you to "trill" the whistle and make different combinations of sounds.

- A **Pealess** whistle is designed for **extreme cold** weather. The pea in a whistle can freeze from the saliva that gets on it at sub zero temperatures. Pealess whistles also tend to be better at making quick blasts of sound.

- The only whistle we have that can produce both a solid tone and a trill is the Dual Tone Whistle. It combines both a pea'ed and pealess whistle.

- **Mega Horns**. Several of the Roy Gonia whistles come in a "Mega" version. These whistles have a **small megaphone** built around them to increase the volume and distance that your dog can hear them. What the mega does is push the sound away from the handler and out toward the dog. These are very loud whistles but they are easier on your ears because of the design.

- **Protect your hearing**: All of the whistles that we sell are loud and any long term exposure to loud sounds can damage your hearing. That said, most folks don't use a whistle enough to do any major damage. We do recommend that you be careful how you use your dog training whistles.

What a Dog Whistle Will NOT Do

The whistles we sell are for **training dogs**. They are used to issue commands and get your dog's attention.

There is **no whistle** that will prevent or **stop a dog from barking**. A whistle may distract the dog from barking for a short period of time but the result in most cases will be temporary. "Annoying" a dog with a whistle is more likely to give a dog something to bark about than to make him stop. An electronic stimulation bark collar is the only effective method for controlling unwanted barking in our opinion.

We get many requests from walkers and joggers looking to keep dogs away with a whistle. We are **not aware** of any whistle that will **repel a dog** or make him leave an area.

We are **not aware** of a whistle that will stop a dog from fighting. As with any loud noise, a whistle might provide a temporary distraction, but it depends on the dog's level of aggression.

We also get requests from folks trying to work with **deaf dogs** and **older dogs** that have some hearing loss. Finding the right whistle depends on the extent of the hearing loss and what range of the dog's hearing is gone (high, low, or midrange). For deaf dogs we recommend a vibration collar for getting their attention and teaching commands with **hand signals**.

Silent Whistles

"Silent" Whistles work just like any other whistles you blow through them and they make a noise. It is called a "silent whistle" because it operates on a **frequency above** that of the average person's hearing. You will hear something, but not much. A few people can hear the actual tone, but most folks just hear the **sound of the air** going through the whistle.

The idea behind this type of whistle is that it will not disturb anyone standing right there with you. Dog's hearing goes further into the ultrasonic range than people so they can hear these whistles. In other words, it is **very LOUD** to dogs but **very QUIET** to people. The whistles are tunable so that you can tune it to a frequency that gets the most response from your dog.

Some dogs do not respond to the frequency range of the silent whistles.

If you want to **minimize the disturbance to others**, go with the silent whistle. Some people will hear it, but most will not.

Acme Thundered and Oblong Whistles

Acme Whistles have been made in England since the late 1800's. They are the oldest whistle company in the world. Acme has pioneered the majority of whistle manufacturing techniques used today.

The Acme Thundered is our number one pointing dog whistle. I grew up using the plastic 558 and 559 as my main training whistles. The Acme Thundered Metal Whistles are also staples in the bird dog world.

Acme Oblong Whistles are a favorite of **close working** retriever trainers and **flushing** dog owners. These whistles are very **easy on the handler's ears** and are popular in situations when you don't need extreme volume.

A pretty common misunderstanding by the general public is that dogs will automatically respond to a whistle with no training. A dog that knows his verbal commands will usually pick up whistle signals very quickly.

If your dog will not obey your verbal commands there is no reason to think he will obey whistle commands.

Without training these whistles are like any other noise to your dog. A whistle command is a cue just like a verbal command. Whistle training is achieved by overlaying the whistle command once the verbal command is mastered.

The first thing you need to do is pick out a standard set of whistle commands. While you can train pretty much any command with a whistle, the normal ones are a recall or "here" command, "sit," and a "change direction" or turn command. The main whistle command in retriever work is the "Sit" whistle which is normally one quick blast. The here or recall whistles can be three or four quick blasts in rapid succession. I use a long trill for a turn whistle. My field dogs are trained to look at me after the turn command is given so I can give a hand signal for the correct direction if needed.

Just like verbal commands, it really does not matter which whistle commands you use, but you must be consistent in your commands. Training with a whistle is just like regular vocal commands, but after the dog learns the command you add the whistle command after the verbal command.

Let's start with the Sit whistle (one quick blast.) You need a dog that has mastered both "heel" and "sit" verbal commands. Start your dog out on a leash in the heel position. As you walk along give the verbal command "Sit" and then immediately blow the whistle. Your dog will sit. Give him verbal praise. Repeat this over and over: verbal command followed with the whistle command. After you have done a certain amount of this, start to drop the verbal command. Only give the verbal command every other time. Once you can see the dog understanding just the whistle command, you can stop giving the verbal.

The same idea applies to all other commands. You will need to have different whistle combinations for every command so that the dog understands which one you want him to do.

FINAL THOUGHTS

There are a variety of silent dog whistles on the market made of different materials.

From a practical standpoint, dog training whistles with a cord attached may turn out helpful because they can be hung in a convenient spot when not in use and worn around the neck when training. Many have an adjustable pitch so they can be tuned to the dog's specific hearing level by loosening the locking nut.

Silent dog whistles are an excellent way to communicate with your dog from a distance without disturbing other people or frightening wildlife. Best of all, the consistency of the whistle tone makes it very effective in delivering clear, easy to understand commands.

Whether you are training your dog to hunt, herd, retrieve or just follow directions from a distance, a silent dog whistle can be advantageous in many ways.

CONCLUSION

In conclusion, as with any other training, whistle training your dog will take some time and you will need plenty of time and patience; do not shout or get impatient with the dog. It is always easier to train a puppy than a grown dog. For smaller dogs, you can use a small dog training whistle which has a higher pitch while for larger dogs, a larger whistle is suitable. There are different types of dog whistles available in plastic or metal.